HARVEY THE HEART
HAD TOO MANY FARTS

ISBN 9798571030588

Harvey the Heart had an interesting problem.
Way too much tooting would blast from his bottom!
He didn't think that his gas was too icky.
But others, he learned, were way much more picky.

A day at the playground could quickly turn sour
when trapped in a toot cloud with toxic smell power.

A picnic was planned in the field by the trees,
but it ended early thanks to his bum breeze.

Library time was for quiet and wonder
until his burrito ignited bum thunder.
His friends would complain when he let his bum groan
that "farting and tooting should be done alone!"

"There has to be someone,"
he cried to the sky,
"who won't run away if I let a
fart fly!"
"Have you met that new girl?"
Timmy inquired.
"Later," said Harvey. "I'm too sad
and tired."

Timmy exclaimed, "She just let out a whopper!"
That got his attention. "Someone please stop her!"

"Wait!" he caught her, "I'm Harvey the Heart.
I have a weird question: did you just fart?"
"I'm Suzie the Circle and yes that was me."
"But you're not embarrassed!" He sighed, "I would be."

She told him, "No bum could be perfectly mute.
We each have a booty! We all need to toot!
I try to be thoughtful and take them outside,
but if one slips out I just take it in stride."

Harvey was shocked! She could fart and feel free?
He tested a toot. Her eyes filled with glee.

"Can you keep a big secret?" she whispered down low,
"I think farting is fun. Would you also say so?"

What did she say?
Did she say she liked tooting?
He pictured her joining in bum canon shooting!
He dreamed of the things they could do with
no fear of the smells and the sounds that could
blow from his rear.

They'd capture their fumes in a
hot air balloon.
They'd soar past the clouds and
go straight to the moon!

Then after their trip through the
sky and the stars,
they'd race at the track in their
gas-powered cars!

How great would life be
with a good friend who knew
all your perks and your quirks
and liked the whole you!

"You still with me?" she asked. His dreams came to an end.
"Oh I'm with you!" he said...

... to his future best friend.

Made in the USA
Middletown, DE
21 November 2022